Simon Peter

THE DISCIPLE

The Story of Simon Peter
accurately retold from the Bible,
(from Matthew, Mark, Luke and John), by
CARINE MACKENZIE

with no pictures of Jesus

Design and Illustrations
Duncan McLaren
Mackay Design Associates Ltd

Published in Great Britain by
CHRISTIAN FOCUS PUBLICATIONS LTD
Geanies House, Fearn, Tain, Ross-shire IV20 1TW, Scotland
http://www.christianfocus.com
© 1983 Christian Focus Publications Ltd ISBN 0 906731 09 7

New edition 1988.
Reprinted 1992
Reprinted 1998
Reprinted 2000

04211

Peter was a special friend of Jesus and worked for Him and so he was called a disciple. Before that he had been a fisherman called Simon, but when he met Jesus his life completely changed; for Jesus made him one of His disciples and gave him his new name, Peter.

Peter saw Jesus doing many wonderful things, some of which you can read about in *"Peter the Fisherman."*

One day Jesus took Peter and two other disciples, James and John up a high mountain to pray. While they were watching, Jesus changed. His face shone as brightly as the sun. His clothes became as white as light. They also saw Moses and Elijah talking with Jesus.

Then a bright cloud covered them and they heard God's voice saying about Jesus, "This is my beloved Son in whom I am well pleased. Hear Him." Peter and the others were so afraid that they fell to the ground but Jesus came over and touched them. When they looked round they saw that Jesus was alone.

Another day, Peter and the other disciples went with Jesus to Jerusalem. They went to the upstairs room of a house to eat a special meal. It was the last meal that Jesus ate with His disciples before He died.

After supper they all went out to the Mount of Olives.

Jesus told them, "You will all be ashamed of me tonight."

Peter answered, "Lord, I will never be ashamed of You, even if everyone else is."

"I am telling you, Peter," Jesus said, "before the cock crows in the morning, you will deny three times that you even know me."

"I would never deny You," exclaimed Peter, "even if I had to die with You."

Peter seemed very brave but he did not realise then how weak he was.

You and I are weak too, just as Peter was. Without Jesus, we can do nothing.

Jesus and His disciples then went into the Garden of Gethsemane.

Jesus asked Peter, James and John to go with Him to a part of the garden and to be on watch for Him while He prayed to His Father in heaven. Jesus knew what great suffering He would soon have and He was very sad.

After He had been praying for a time, Jesus came back to Peter and the other two disciples and found them all sleeping.

He said to Peter, "Could you not watch with me for one hour?"

Jesus went to pray again and when He came back the second time He found them all asleep again. After they had fallen asleep a third time, Jesus said, "You can sleep on now."

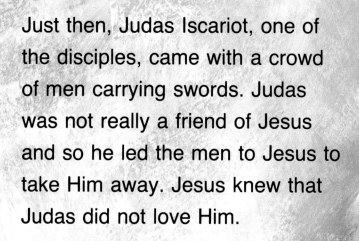

Just then, Judas Iscariot, one of the disciples, came with a crowd of men carrying swords. Judas was not really a friend of Jesus and so he led the men to Jesus to take Him away. Jesus knew that Judas did not love Him.

Jesus knows too if you love Him or not. Ask God to give you love in your heart for Jesus.

When the men grabbed Jesus to take Him away, Peter took a sword and struck one of the men and cut off his ear. Jesus turned to Peter and said, "Put your sword away. We do not need to fight with swords. If I wanted to, I could ask God for thousands of angels to help me." Jesus healed the man's ear immediately.

Then all the disciples, even Peter, ran away and left Jesus alone. The wicked men took Jesus to the palace of Caiaphas, the High Priest.

Peter then began to follow them at a distance. He went right into the palace and sat down with the servants around a fire in the middle of the hall. He wanted to know what would happen to Jesus.

A girl went to Peter and said, "Were you not one of those who went about with Jesus of Galilee?" Peter answered, "I do not know what you are talking about."

Then he went out to the porch and another girl saw him and said to the people there, "This fellow was with Jesus of Nazareth too." Peter denied this again. "I do not know the man," he said.

After a short time a man said to Peter, "Surely you are one of Jesus' followers, for you speak like them."

Peter spoke roughly and said, "I do not know the man."

Immediately the cock crew. Jesus turned round and looked at Peter. Peter then remembered that Jesus had said, "Before the cock crows, you shall deny me three times." Peter had been so sure that he would stand by Jesus, but he failed. He had denied his Master. Peter was so sad and upset that he went outside and cried very much.

We need Jesus to keep us from doing wrong. If we think that we can do what is right without Him then we will fail badly like Peter.

Jesus was cruelly treated. The soldiers made a crown of thorns and put it on His head. They mocked Him and spat on Him and they hit Him on the head with a stick. Then they took Him to Calvary and nailed Him to a cross of wood. There He died.

Why did this happen to Jesus? God must punish sin. Jesus took that punishment Himself in the place of people who trust in Him. Boys and girls who trust in the Lord Jesus have all their sins forgiven and will be made fit for heaven at the end of their lives. That is why Jesus died.

Peter was not there when Jesus died on the cross. How sad and ashamed he must have felt.

Jesus' body was laid in a grave called a sepulchre. Some ladies, who loved Jesus, went to the sepulchre. They looked inside and saw an angel sitting there and they were afraid.

The angel said, "Do not be afraid. You are looking for Jesus who was crucified: He is risen: He is not here. Go and tell his disciples and Peter that He is going to Galilee and you will all see Him there."

Peter and John could hardly believe that Jesus was not in the grave. They wanted to see for themselves so they ran as fast as they could to the sepulchre. They saw the empty grave and the grave clothes lying neatly folded. They believed now what the women had told them. Jesus' body was not in the grave. Peter and John went back home.

That evening the disciples met together in a room with the doors tightly shut. They were afraid that the people would kill them too. A really wonderful thing happened. Jesus came into the room although the doors were shut. He spoke to them. "Peace be to you," He said. Jesus showed them His hands which had been pierced by the nails on the cross, and His side which had been pierced by a spear. Peter and the rest of the disciples were so glad when they saw Jesus.

One evening some time later, Peter and some other disciples were together on the shore of the sea of Galilee. Peter said, "I am going to fish." "We will go with you," said the others. They went out in a boat and fished all night but they caught nothing.

When the morning came they saw a man on the shore watching them. He asked them, "Have you any food?" "No," they replied. He then told them, "Put the net out on the right side of the boat and you will find fish." When they did this the net became so full of fish that they could not pull it into the boat.

Then John knew that the person on the shore was Jesus. "It is the Lord," he said to Peter. Peter pulled on his fisherman's coat and dived into the water to swim to the shore. He was so eager to reach Jesus that he could not wait for the boat to sail ashore.

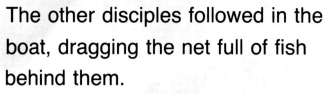

The other disciples followed in the boat, dragging the net full of fish behind them.

When they came ashore, they saw that Jesus had a meal of fish and bread ready for them on a fire.

Jesus said to them, "Bring the fish that you have now caught." Peter pulled the net ashore and they counted the catch; one hundred and fifty three big fish.

Although there was such a great and heavy catch of fish the net was not broken at all.

"Come and eat," said Jesus. He handed round the bread and fish. When they had finished eating Jesus turned to Peter and, using his other name, said, "Simon, do you love me?" "Yes Lord, You know that I love You," Peter answered. "Feed my lambs," Jesus said to him.

Again Jesus said, "Simon, do you love me?" "Yes Lord, You know that I love You," Peter answered again. "Feed my sheep," said Jesus.

Jesus asked the same question again, "Simon do you love me?" Peter was upset at being asked a third time and he said to Jesus, "Lord, You know everything. You know that I love You." "Feed my sheep," Jesus told him.

Peter had now said three times that he loved Jesus. Perhaps he remembered with shame that he had denied Jesus three times in the past. But Jesus had forgiven him. He wanted Peter to feed His lambs and sheep. Jesus meant that He wanted Peter to preach the gospel to the people. Peter obeyed Jesus and became a great and fearless preacher of the Gospel.